D1129030

THE LIFE STORIES *of* PEE PAW

MATTHEW RUCKER

ISBN: 978-1-7339158-0-9   [Paperback Edition]
      978-1-7339158-1-6   [Hardback Edition]
      978-1-7339158-2-3   [eBook Edition]

Printed and bound in The United States of America.

Published by

The Mulberry Books, LLC.
8330 E Quincy Avenue, Denver CO 80237
themulberrybooks.com

CONTENTS

ACKNOWLEDGEMENTS

L et me first of all thank my dear wife, Angela, who encouraged me to do this book. Without her none of this would have happened. Also, let me thank my family, friends, and church members who provided the stories. Thank you for allowing me to be a part of those stories.

INTRODUCTION

In the ministry I found so many grandchildren didn't know their grandparents. They knew some facts about them but really didn't know them. So I wrote a book of stories about me for my granddaughter. These stories give an insight into who I am. It may not mean much now but in later years I think she will appreciate it. I have included the good as well as the bad times. I didn't want the book to be one sided but let her know I had struggles along the way. I also always tried to give insight to Alyssa in some of the stories. So enjoy the true stories of PeePaw from my birth to present day.

I GREW UP ON A FARM

We had chickens, which we used for eggs and meat. We had hogs that we sold and butchered some to have meat and to share with neighbors. We had cows, which we used for milk and meat. Every fall we would butcher a cow. Another cow would be milked every day, and the milk would stand overnight, when it would be ready to skim the cream off the top. This cream was used to churn into butter.

Crops were grown and cultivated with a mule (plowing a mule is one heck of a task; they had a mind of their own). The mule was used to prepare the land, plant the crops, cultivate the crops; he was also used with a grain drill and side cutter to cut hay.

In the fall we hauled hay to the barn to put up in the loft and cornstalks (called fodder) to feed the cattle and the mule in the winter.

The corn was broken by hand, shucked, and shelled to use as feed for the animals. Some of the corn was taken to the mill in Swansea and ground into grits and cornmeal that was used in cooking. We canned our vegetables (my grandmother taught me how) and made our own syrup (sugarcane) with the mill that I still have. In the fall of the year, of course we made sauerkraut.

We cut our wood with an ax and a crosscut saw to cook and warm with. Later Dad bought a chainsaw that was so heavy it would break your back cutting with it. In the winter gathering firewood was a daily chore.

We salt-cured our meat (in the smokehouse, which I use now as my toolshed) and processed our dried beans.

The processing of the beans consisted of putting dried beans in a sack and putting them out in the sun and beating them with a stick several times a day. I can still hear those beans and peas popping when they got warm in the sun. After several days we would remove the hulls and wait for the wind to blow and then hold a bucket of peas or beans as high as you could in the air, waiting for the wind to blow the husk out as you poured them into a tin tub. By the way, my first bathtub was a big tin tub because we didn't have a bathroom.

Alyssa, you see, we were self-efficient in a sense that involved a lot of work, lots of work. Yet it shaped me into the man I became in this life. Never fear hard work, but always fear being lazy. I am glad I grew up on a farm.

MY BIRTH

I was the firstborn of my family, and Mom had a hard delivery. She was in labor for hours; when I finally came, I was blue, and survival was a concern.

My granddad (BooPaw) went to the house where Angela and I now live and prayed for me to live. In the process of praying, he told God that if He let me live, then he would give me to God.

Mom told me this story and always believed God had His hand on me. I know I have felt His presence many times.

Now Mom had this gift to know something was going to happen. She would amaze me with some of the things she could predict. She only shared this with people close to her, one also being my wife.

My faith is strong, and I too can sense things. It just comes to me, and I share a lot with Angela. I have walked into rooms in a hospital and get this feeling they were going to die. I remember a time sitting in my friend's hospital room one night, and the thought went through my mind, "He's going to die." Next morning he had a heart attack and died.

Sometimes I can sense something is going to happen in someone's life. I don't know what, but something will happen. I think this is all a part of my life because my BooPaw gave me to God.

Matthew Rucker

BUTCHERING A HOG

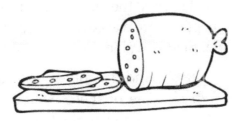

utchering a hog—or should I say *hogs*—was always on Thanksgiving Day, and with my uncles bringing some, we may end up butchering ten or twelve.

The day of the butchering began early about 5:00 a.m., with starting a fire around pots of water. A fifty-five-gallon drum was dug into the ground at an angle. Boards were placed on the ground in front of the barrel to keep the hog off the ground. The hogs (usually two at a time) were shot and boiling water added to drum. Soap powder was added as well.

Now to test the heat of the water, take your pointing finger and cut it through the water in the drum; if you could do it only one or two times, the water is too hot. If you could cut through the water four times, it is too cold. What you are looking for is to be able to cut your finger through the water three times, and no more. If the water is too hot or too cold, you would set the hair on the hog (hair wouldn't pull out).

The hog was placed in the barrel and then pulled out to catch air, and we began pulling the hair off it. We then scraped the hog, and it was pretty and white. It was then ready to be hung up to wash and then gut.

The tendons in the back legs were exposed, and a hickory stick was placed between the two hind feet, and the hog was pulled up into the air. The head was then removed and the hog cut open to release the innards. The liver, kidneys, heart, and intestines were separated.

The head was cut up, and the pudding pot began. The head, onions, salt, and pepper were placed in a washpot with water. It cooked for a while, then liver, kidneys, and heart were added.

The hog was cut up, and my job was to salt the hams, shoulders, and fatback. One of these would be cooked for Christmas Day. Meat trimmed from the hams, shoulders, and etc. was laid aside. The lean meat went to make sausage while the fat was to be used for cooking grease or lard.

My second job was to clean the intestines. I was the water pourer. Pearly, a black lady, cut them the proper links, and we would wash them out. They were placed then in lime-water mixture to soak. After several hours, they were scraped.

The lean meat was ground for sausage and the fat for lard. The pudding pot contents were also ground. The sausage was seasoned with onion, salt, pepper, and spices. It was then stuffed with a stuffer into the small intestines.

The ground pudding pot contents were mixed with salt, pepper, spices, and rice and stuffed into the large intestines. Then sausage was hung on racks in the smokehouse to dry.

The pudding was placed back in pudding pot juice to cook. This would tighten them up. The whole pot after they were done was placed in the smokehouse. Later they were put in the freezer.

We were now ready to complete the day by frying the lard. This was a slow constant stirring job. After it fried out, it was poured in cans sitting in water to cool. It would look like white Crisco. This would be used throughout the year for frying and making bread.

Now remember this was one hog, and we would have ten or more. It was a day, and neighbors who helped would get a mess of sausage, pudding, and fresh pork.

Now, Alyssa, I do believe if kids saw this today, they wouldn't eat pork, but remember this was a way of life for me. Butchering a hog provided food for us to survive, and all of that was normal for me.

BOOPAW, THE MULE, AND ME

Sitting on my man's cave porch, I can look toward the interstate and see what is left of old terraces (fields on different levels). There were the terraces, and my granddad planted corn on each one. Now these fields were worked by a mule that Granddad had.

In the spring, Granddad, who I called *BooPaw*, would plow the land up with his mule. As a boy I would walk behind barefooted in the furrows. The cool dirt felt good on my feet. Corn was planted and later cultivated. The sun would rise up in the sky, and that mule would work.

In the fall it was time to harvest the corn by hand (of course) and brought to the barn for the animals. Corn was shelled by hand for the cows, hogs, chickens, and mule. This was the yearly cycle.

Those were good times with my BooPaw. Now as I sit home on the porch of my man cave looking down across the terraces, I go back in my mind, and I can feel the fresh turned dirt between my toes and see BooPaw, the mule, and me.

DAD BUYS A TRACTOR

Dad bought a Farmall tractor to make things easier. He had retired the mule, and she finally died, and I spent a lot of time on the tractor: disking up the land, planting, cultivating (plowing the crops), and harvesting. If you want to experience a long day, get on a tractor at daylight and get off at sunset.

It was still hard work, and during the week, my dad would come in my room before he went to work and tell me what he wanted me to do after school. This was in addition to my regular chores. I can still hear him telling me, "Buckshot, get your brother to help you." The hardest thing about this was that Dad wanted me to take charge of my brother helping with the assigned chores. He is lucky to be alive today, because there were many days I could have killed him because he was so stubborn (I still want to kill him sometimes now).

We used the tractor to haul firewood for heating and cooking, to haul straw to put in the stables, and haul manure out of the stables to spread on the field during springtime.

You know, Alyssa, I still enjoy riding a tractor, and I will go to my grave loving that. If I could be buried on my tractor, I would be happy.

MY FIRST DOG

My first dog was named Junior. He was a cross between a German shepherd and a hound dog. He was my friend.

We played together, especially in an old iron bathtub under the pecan trees. It was our ship, and we sailed the seven seas. We fought sea monsters and captured many islands. Now I'm not sure Junior was as thrilled as I was, especially being loaded in and out the boat to fight.

*****

It was one of those cold fall days, and Dad had to cut wood for the fire. I wanted to help, so I jumped in the trailer. We came to the place to cut the tree, and Junior had followed us down.

Dad told me to hold him while he cut the tree down. I held him tight until just as the tree started falling, and he broke free running in the path of the falling tree. It crashed down on him. Dad came over and cut the limbs off him, but it was too late. Junior was dead. Dad picked him up and laid him by a big tree as I cried.

Dad kneeled down and hugged me and said, "Buckshot, death is a part of life, and you will see a lot of it in your life. I know you hurt for your dog, but life goes on. It's okay to cry, but you have two choices: you can stay here by the tree and cry, or you can get up and help me with the wood and we'll go home. I know you hurt, but life goes on. I'm here for you, and we'll get you another dog."

Alyssa, in the ministry, I've had many visits with death—from the very young to the very old. In my own family and close friends, it has come. I learned to cry in private and go on with life. Sure it hurts, but I learned you couldn't stay by the tree. I had to go on with life. It was hard doing my mom's funeral—so hard, but my son's funeral was unbearable. Part of me died that day, but I remember his last words for me as he got out of the truck at school that morning, "Dad, you are the coolest dad, and know that I love you." I got knocked down but not knocked out.

I remember the words of my dad under that hickory tree: you can stay here, or get up and move on. Even in death, my first dog, Junior, taught me to face death, an old friend in my life. Thank you, Dad and Junior.

SPECIAL TREATS

As a family, we never had much money, and little things were treats. I remember going to Aunt Gladys's store (to everyone today, it is Pete's store).

There were two things that I got at the store; one was if a certain uncle was there, I would get a cinnamon roll from him. Now he would buy me a cinnamon roll just to watch me eat it. These rolls had raisins on them, and for some reason, I thought they were flies. He used to laugh and watch me pick the raisins off and throw them on the ground before I ate it. I later learned they were not flies and began to eat them.

The other thing that I would get was a lollipop. There is something about having a stick sticking out your mouth with candy on the other end. At that moment in time, I was the "tomcat's kitten," and life was good.

A lollipop was a special treat when I was younger, so always appreciate the little things in life. It may not seem much, but with the right spirit, it can change you to be thankful for them.

So, Alyssa, grab a lollipop and keep in mind that it is 721 licks to the chocolate center.

THE NAIL

When I was very young, my grandmother taught me to write my ABCs. Then one day she taught me to write my name, *Matt*. I was so proud! I couldn't wait to show Mom and Dad. They were going to be so proud of me.

Burton International delivered a new truck to my dad, a light blue one. I came up with the idea after I found an old rusty nail, I could write my name on the door for Mom and Dad to see. Carefully I wrote M-A-T- T. It looked so good.

Mom would be the first home, so I watched for her. She arrived and so excited I told her I had something to show her. Arriving at the truck and proudly said, "I wrote my name!" A hush fell upon Mom, and when she finally spoke, she said, "Your dad is going to kill you." I heard her, but I still thought my dad would be proud.

Well, Dad came home from work, and Mom was right. He whipped me for scratching his truck's door. He wasn't proud.

I had done what I thought would be good, but it turned out bad. That's the way it goes sometimes in life. Alyssa, you may think it is good, but it can turn out bad. For example, lying for a friend or taking just one piece of candy or cheating on a test to pass the course are all bad.

And when you get older, things such as lying to your mate because you don't want to hurt them or taking a drink to be a part of the crowd, and it doesn't stop. Giving to your children everything they want and not saying no. They aren't taught limits, and the good things you give don't help but hurt the child.

You know I don't think I deserved that whipping. I did it with the right spirit, not hate or anger, just to make my parents proud. Yet I shouldn't have taken a nail and scratched Dad's new truck. Hey, it wasn't my fault, it was the nail's, and that's a whole new story.

LEARNING TO HUNT

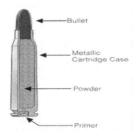

Bullet

Metallic
Cartridge Case

Powder

Primer

My first gun that I learned to shoot was a .22 rifle, and I was always practicing. I am sure if this land was shifted on top of this hill, God would only know how much lead is buried here. As I grew older, I became a good shot, which led me to become an expert marksman in the military. I could shoot a rat running or a duck flying.

I remember the first time that I shot a shotgun. Knowing that it would kick, I went down into the woods by myself and sat down by a tree and put the butt up against the tree and pulled the trigger. I ran to the house to let my dad know that I had fired the gun.

He praised me for shooting the gun, but I never told him that I lied about it. This is the only time that I lied to my dad. But in the following months, I learned to shoot the shotgun, and it was a natural thing for me. To give you an example, shooting doves out of a box of 24, my brother would get one, and I would get 15 plus or more. Hunting was very much a part of my life growing up, which provided meat for the table. I hunted squirrel, rabbit, possum, coon, and deer. I also hunted duck, quail, dove, and turkey.

Alyssa, today my guns of choice are a pellet gun with scope and a BB gun, and you better not mess with this old man 'cause he can still shoot.

So learn to shoot good, and maybe one day we will go squirrel hunting, and you can get one, and we will cook it and eat it together. Oh, happy days!

A DOG'S BEST FRIEND

As kids, my dad had a bulldog that he kept chained in the front yard. He was chained because he would bite. In fact if my brother and I got within the chain, he wouldn't let anyone get to us except my dad or mom.

Now my brother got within the reach of the chain and was playing with Bully. Maybe my brother was playing too hard or pulled his tail, and Bully snapped at him. The next thing I knew, Jimmy, my brother, bit down on Bully's ear; and all Bully did was sit there and whine. Jimmy wouldn't let go, and Dad had to get Jimmy away from him.

Now Bully from then on would avoid Jimmy each time he came around. That was a characteristic of my brother—he would bite. He would bite man, child, or beast, even man's best friend.

Alyssa, you will find in this life that people who bark (talk too much) will also bite you (hurt you with words). If you talk too much, you will end up saying the wrong thing and hurting someone. Make sure your brain is in gear and your tongue is in neutral before you speak. That makes you a wise person.

YOU KILLED MY BROTHER

I was fifteen months older than my brother. We played together under the house with toy tractors and trucks.

As we grew older, one Christmas morning, Mom and Dad gave us cap pistols. They were cowboy pistols with holsters. A roll of caps was placed in them, and they would make a loud bang. Boy, did we have fun with those especially with the cats.

My grandmother forbid us to shoot these in the house because it scared her. But we forgot, and while in the kitchen, my brother fired at me. Granny grabbed the pistol from him and hit him in the head. He started bleeding, and it could be seen easily because our hair was always short.

Seeing the blood, I cried out, "You have killed my brother!" Granny, now concerned, took a washcloth with ice in it to stop the bleeding. When she would check it, a small trickle of blood mixed with water could be seen. Again each time when she would look, I would cry out, "You have killed my brother!" She would say, "He's okay, he'll be fine."

Again I would remind Granny he was bleeding to death and that she had killed him.

Eventually my brother didn't die, and I doubt if any scar can be seen. I'm glad he lived to see another day. We never shot the pistols in the house again because of the day when Granny tried to kill my brother.

WHO SCARED WHO?

It was Halloween, and we boys were bored. There must be something we could do that was exciting.

We decided we would scare a local family with several children. I got one of Mom's pillowcases and a fishing cane. I tied the pillowcase to the end of the pole, and voila, a ghost.

It was so dark as my cousin and I approached the house. We crawled on our stomachs up to the window. It was showtime, and we fought back laughing as we raised the ghost in front of the window. We heard them scream, and we ran down to a plumb thicket and lay down with me on top of the ghost.

They came out with guns a blasting shooting down across the field. They would point a light, and if they saw anything suspicious, they would shoot. Unknown to them they were shooting over us, and we could hear the bullets flying through the air. After a while they went back in the house. It was time to *run*.

My cousin and I took off down across my uncle's watermelon patch. Now, cuz was scared and started crying. I was behind with the cane and the ghost. I realized that I wouldn't make it to the woods in time, so I hit the ground. I went headfirst into one of those big watermelons. My first thought was that I had busted my head open. I lay there thinking the worst because I was afraid to move. Shots were fired again, and when silence returned, I hit the woods knowing my head hadn't busted.

Alyssa, people play jokes and pranks on people. Something can seem to be funny and that no one will get hurt, but you can hurt them or yourself. As you go through life, especially the teenage years, people will invite you to do crazy things. I only ask that you think about it first. Something as simple as a pole and pillowcase at Halloween could have gotten me killed.

MOM'S MACARONI

Y ou might say we lived in the woods with no one around. It was open space.

The dogs were allowed to run free, and every evening they would begin to play in the yard and soon disappear into the woods. I remember getting up with Dad and listening for the dogs. Hearing them we would head out.

Now Dad's dogs were his pride and joy, especially Old Stonewall. He was like the trainer of the rest in the yard. Dad really loved Stonewall.

Now one of our favorite foods was mac and cheese (not out of a box). Food left over was given to the dogs, and they would gather around the back steps if Mom stepped out with a pot. Today's feast was macaroni with cheese. Mom threw it into the air, and the dogs froze. Stonewall jumped into the air and caught it and tried to gobble it down. He tried to suck air but failed and fell over dead.

When Dad came home, Stonewall was still lying in the yard. Dad asked what happened to him. I told him that Mama threw out some macaroni, and he grabbed it and fell over.

My dad was hot, and he told my mom to never make macaroni and cheese again. Mom ceased making it, and the only way we got some was at other people's houses.

But, Alyssa, I believe if Stonewall wasn't so greedy, he wouldn't have died, and Mom could have continued making macaroni and cheese. Remember, Alyssa, to always share, don't be greedy, it'll get you in trouble every time.

LITTLE HENRY

My coon hunting buddy was Paul. His dad was the milker at the dairy close to our home.

Now this diary had about one hundred cows that milked and two bulls, Little Henry and Big Henry. The bulls each weighed about 2,000 lbs., and Little Henry was mean. We would find out where he was before we hunted an area. Getting that information, the hunt was on.

It was one of those cold moonlit nights, and it wasn't long before the dogs struck a coon (found a trail where one had walked). They finally treed, and we started to the tree.

We came to a fence and climbed over thinking we were safe. Walking out across the pasture, I thought I heard a cow. Paul assured me the cows were in the other pasture. We approached a tree in the pasture as we continued for the other side. As we came closer to the tree, I saw movement, and then as my eyes focused, I heard Little Henry *bellow*. He started toward us. Now you can talk of world records in track, but on that night, I broke them all. I was running to the fence with Little Henry in hot pursuit. As I came to the fence, another world record, and I sailed over it.

Now Little Henry bellowed and pawed, and the macho in me came out. "I beat you, ha, I beat you." It's amazing how brave we become on the other side of the fence.

Alyssa, in this life there are many dangers, but always remember God will provide a fence.

THE SANDY RUN CREEK

An important place in my life was the Sandy Run Creek. The water is so cold that it refreshes you so on a hot day. It was a simple spring-fed creek that we customized. First, we cut a tree across it to cause the water to wash out a hole. So now instead of two feet deep, it was six, but that caused a problem.

Someone had to jump in first to scare the snakes out. The first jump was made quickly to avoid the snakes. The hole was down the creek a ways hidden from the road. Therefore, swimwear was not required; in fact, very seldom did any of us have one.

On the far side of the creek was a stump on which lay a bar of soap, ivory, which had to be replaced after each flood. We left the creek clean but wet. No towels were present, so we put back on our clothes to soak up the water.

The creek was also a healing area. If you felt bad, just jump into the cooling water, and things felt better. When you emerged from the water, your lips were blue and you felt better. Lots of the good memories were made at the creek.

Alyssa, everybody needs a fun place in life where you can act like a kid again. This is a place where everybody is on the same level and problems float away. Riding is probably your place, but I would love to take you to my place and throw you in and see your lips turn blue. It doesn't get any better than that at my creek.

WEST SHOWS UP

The Highway Patrol Officer is West, Butch and T are my cousins, La La and Nate are my friends, and my brother Jimmy and I—we are the characters of this story.

La La, Butch, Jimmy, and I are riding motorcycles. Butch and Jimmy are riding my cycle, and I am riding behind La La on his. Everything is going fine other than riding them on the main highway. That was a no-no.

All of a sudden Officer West passes us and turns around, puts on his blue light. We haul butt and quickly turn onto a dirt road. Jimmy and Butch are ahead, and I come up with a plan. I tell La La that I was going to jump off and for him to keep on going.

Now have you ever jumped off a motorcycle running 50 mph in a sand bed? Well, I did, and I didn't think I would ever stop rolling even down through the trees. I had sand everywhere. Jimmy and Butch cut down through the woods laying the bike down and running.

We all got away, and La La went home, and Jimmy, Butch, and I walked to our house. When we get there, Nate is there, and we tell him our story. He laughs and tells us how Officer West would have never caught him, and he said, "I would go get the bike and dare Officer West to try and stop me." We tried to tell him Officer West was still in the area, but that seemed to inspire him more. He was going to show us how it was done. We dropped him off on the dirt road, and he went to retrieve the bike.

Meanwhile, my cousin T was watering the grass in his front yard, just a great afternoon. All of a sudden he hears a motorcycle coming up his driveway with a big Crown Vic behind him with sirens and lights going. Up across T's yard, past the house, up the terraces to woods behind his house they went. They dropped across the hill, and soon it was deathly quiet. In a short while the Crown Vic comes back over the hill, and sitting in the backseat is Nate.

You see, Nate didn't know Uncle Woodrow had put up a hog fence across the road that normally would have given access to hundreds of acres. Nate had been caught.

Meanwhile, all of us were at our house along with Nate's dad. The big Crown Vic pulls in the yard, and Officer West asks for Nate's dad. They talked a while, and Nate's dad wasn't too happy especially when he had to pay $125 to Officer West. It was a hard evening for Nate after he bragged so much about what he could do, but Officer West showed him.

Alyssa, I've seen people brag about what they can do and then can't produce. Be careful doing things that are wrong because you will get caught, and that's no fun. Don't let your mouth overload you. Don't think you are better than you are, you will never be superwoman. You see, Nate let his mouth overload him, and he couldn't produce when Officer West showed up.

A MAN I LOOKED UP TO

U ncle Ed was a man I looked up to my whole life. He was a quiet man, a thinker. He had his college degree, and I too wanted to achieve that. Not only to please him but also my dad, who only went as high as the eighth grade. These were the two men who drove me to college.

I have always been a thinker, and I learned a lot from being around Uncle Ed. When I would work with him, he always encourages me to think before doing. That mind-set shaped me in life, my theology, and the role of the minister I became.

When I was in seminary and would come home, Uncle Ed would always give me a check to help out in school. It was always between the two of us. His only comment was for me to help others in life, pay it forward. He would always tell me, "I'm proud of you, son." I loved him so.

The last great gift I was able to give to him was officiating at his funeral. It was easy to preach at his funeral because he had lived a life that had touched so many, evident by the crowd at the funeral. He was a role model to many, and many loved him. He was a role model for me, and I must confess I inherited some of his qualities, qualities of which I am proud.

Alyssa, we all need role models in life to shape our character. Now the world offers a lot of them, but many are shallow. They can't stand the test of time, and they fall by the roadside. I would challenge you to look for someone who is stable, genuine, and well-grounded. By grounded I mean the person who can hold steady when the storms of life come. They endure the storm and face it head-on with a faith. They don't run away. I always looked for faith in an individual. Therefore, my greatest role model is Jesus Christ, and since Uncle Ed had Christ in his heart, he became a man that I looked up to.

FOCUS ON THE TASK, NOT TALK

ome of my best times were fishing with my Uncle Ed. He was a quiet man and believed we had to sneak up on the fish. We had to be quiet putting the boat into the water. We had to be quiet in the boat as we traveled across the water. No loud talking was allowed. Uncle Ed paddled the boat from the front seat of the boat. The paddle didn't come out of the water but made a gentle swirling motion pulling the boat along. When he spoke, it was in a small mumbling fashion. All I would hear would be a mumbling, and he would turn and look at me. I would reply, "Yes, sir," not knowing a word he said. He would mumble something else as he pointed to a cove. I again would answer, "Yes, sir." I never heard a clear word across that lake, yet I would answer, "Yes, sir." I don't know what I was agreeing to, but the task at hand was to catch fish.

Alyssa, this kind of communication isn't bad because it didn't hurt anyone. But sometimes people hear what they want to hear then take that to hurt other people. We call that gossip. Be careful spreading gossip about other people. Make sure you get the facts straight, and by the way, many times it's none of your business in the first place. I live by the philosophy that if you can't say something good about someone, don't say it. Now, I'm sure Uncle Ed enjoyed our conversation more than me. He knew what was being said. Maybe by answering to what I didn't know was a lie, but we always caught fish.

Alyssa, leave most of what you hear in a conversation on the table. How much is true, how much is foolishness, how much is uplifting, and how much needs to be repeated. I have also lived by the philosophy of watching a person's actions, not so much the words they say. My dad put it right when he said, "Never listen to someone tell you of how to plant your garden until you see theirs." "I can't hear a word you're saying by what you're doing," I remind people in counseling. I encourage people to focus on the task at hand, not the words being said, and success is yours. Good fishing, my dear.

THROWING CHERRY BOMBS

y brother, cousin, and I loved to hunt. We found out the wood ducks were flying into a neighbor's pond. In order to fly into the pond, they had to fly over my uncle's land. All we had to do was stand in the branch and shoot them as they came in for a landing. They flew in because our neighbor, a judge, baited the ducks in his pond with corn. We shot for a few evenings and killed some ducks. Then one evening as we waited on the ducks to fly, a game warden showed up. He told us that we couldn't shoot the ducks, for they were the judge's ducks.

He threatened to fine us if we didn't leave. Even though we were on my uncle's land who gave us permission, we were told we had to leave.

Now this didn't sit well with us, for we knew we were in the right, so we decided to get even. What could we do to even the score? My cousin came up with idea that we blow up his mailbox. So we got ready. We bought some of those cherry bombs and waited for dark. Firing up my Volkswagen bug, we set out.

My cousin lit up a cigar, and we were ready to put the plan in action. Pulling up to the box, my cousin opened the mailbox and lit the bomb. Now, instead of carefully throwing it into the mailbox and shutting the lid, he throws it at the box. It hit the rim of the mailbox and bounces back into the bug's back seat.

Have you ever heard a cherry bomb explode in a Volkswagen bug while you are sitting in it? It's no fun to experience it. Our ears rang for several days and just hurt. It didn't work out like we had planned. Judge, two; Matt and cuz a zero was the final score

Alyssa, we can do some crazy things in life and get hurt. I've seen people ride a horse with a saddle and then think they are an Indian and try to ride bareback.

I've seen those people get hurt because of that stupidity. Always think before doing something stupid. Think before you do. You see we had a great plan, and what could go wrong? We were going to get even. What we didn't figure was the cherry bomb being a quarter inch too far right, causing it to hit the rim and bounce back. Always be careful trying to get even because there are no guaranties you will. Be careful throwing stones—or in this case a cherry bomb.

Matthew Rucker

A POCKETBOOK OF HORNETS

My mom always had a large pocketbook that had everything in it, including the kitchen sink. She bought a new one and threw the old one out on the porch. My mind began to think what I could do with this large pocketbook. No answer came.

That night I went coon hunting with Mr. Tillis and Mr. Petty behind our house. While hunting we came upon a large hornet's nest hanging low on a limb, and my mind kicked in again, and I thought I could put the nest in that pocketbook. I would come back the next night and get it.

The following day when darkness occurred, I set out to capture it. Carefully I eased the pocketbook over the nest and broke it off. I quickly shut the lid, and I had them. So what do I do now? The next day I found out that if I shook them, they would just hum. It was so cool.

My mind kicked in gear again. What if someone tried to steal this purse? They would get just what they deserved. But how could I set this up for a thief? Ah, the interstate ran on the edge of our property with lots of cars. Surely someone would try and steal it if I placed it on the side of the road.

Armed with a pocketbook full of hornets, I walked to the interstate. I eased up on the side of the road to see if all was clear. The interstate didn't have the flow of traffic as it has now. All clear, so I gave it one last shake and placed it on the side of the road.

Before too long, a Ford Fairlane station wagon from New Jersey slammed on the brakes and pulled over. There were seven young men, and one jumped out looking both ways, grabbed the pocketbook, and then jumped back in the station wagon. They squealed the tires, and off they went. About thirty yards, the brake slammed, and all four doors and the tailgate open. They emerge beating the air with their arms. Those fellows could really move.

They finally get a stick and removed the pocketbook, and after a while, they loaded up, and off they went. It was the funniest thing I had ever seen. They tried to steal a pocketbook, and when it was opened, I knew those hornets were saying, "Just give me something to bite," and they did. I thought they got what they deserved.

Alyssa, sometimes PeePaw's brain acts a little crazy. I have a vivid imagination that comes up with some crazy things to do. Remember you have some of me in you, so be careful.

You see, I never thought of the danger in all of this, but what if they got up to speed and then opened it? What normal kid would come up with this plan of how to use a large pocketbook, filled with hornets? I know I'm a little bit crazy, but maybe they learned not to snatch another purse. Maybe I taught them a lesson, and just between me and you, it was funny.

RODEO MATT

We had a young bull around five hundred pounds ready for market. It was shut up in a stable when the trailer arrived. My friend Marion asked if I was going to load him. And at a ripe old age of fifteen, I responded, "I got him."

For some stupid reason, I decided to catch him. Now have you ever grabbed hold of a five-hundred-pound bull? Once you grab him, it is hard to let him go. My arms around his neck, he slammed me into every wall. He used me to tear down Dad's homemade hayrack. I was wallowed on the ground in all the cow manure, but I held on tight. I finally wrestled him down, which seemed like half a day, and got a rope on him. We then pulled him onto the trailer. They asked me, "Are you hurt?" Macho me wounded and bleeding proudly responded, "I had him all the time."

The next day I was sore, could hardly move, but I rubbed down with liniment, not letting on how I really was feeling. I had been in a fight, and I had won.

By the way, several years later, I had the opportunity to grab a young horse, and that was an adventure. I gave the rodeo up after that.

Alyssa, animals can hurt us, and sometimes because we are stupid and do stupid things. Always use your head around them. I would never try to grab a five-hundred-pound bull now, but at fifteen, no problem. I've seen it done on television, so let the rodeo begin, open the chute, but don't let your mouth overload your ability.

MY FIRST LOVE

Ah, first love, it defies explanation. You might say it is a form of madness, and it consumes a person. Such was my experience with first love.

It happened in a strange way. I had to sponsor someone for homecoming for the football team. I was now a senior, and I asked this girl in the class if she would be my sponsor. She said yes, and she was my first date. It turned out to be a short night, and I took her home. Of course I had to go in to see all the family. It was then that my eye focused on her baby sister. I thought she was the most beautiful thing I had ever seen. I couldn't get her out of my mind. So after having one date under my belt, I was ready. I had broken the ice on this dating thing.

I went to see her mom and asked if I could date her daughter. She was hoeing in the garden, and she listened and said, "I would be proud to have you date my daughter." I asked her out that Friday night, and that was our first date.

This relationship lasted for six years. It was the springtime of my life, and all was good. Love and happiness grew stronger. We even talked about the future and a life together. Everything was great, and by the way, sex never entered in.

I was in college studying for my MBA at University of South Carolina. After I graduated, we talked about building on her dad's land. We even picked the spot. Life was good.

It was then I felt the call to the ministry (another story), and the pull was so great I had to walk that path. She and I always did church work together. She could play the piano and sing, it all seemed so perfect.

But then the storms of life began to gather, and a separation took place. I still don't know why the relationship ended. Was it something I said or did to cause it to end? That question still haunts me some fifty years later. So as quick as it started, it ended just as quick. I know it crushed me, and yet a part of me still loves her. She was my first love.

Alyssa, you will have a first love, and you will go crazy. It will be like nothing you have experienced before. Your mom will want to kill you. I probably will too. But always remember I understand, for I have been there.

Guard your heart, for first loves rarely last, and the hurt is so great. It may work out, so don't be afraid. Move ahead and trust that God will take care of you if it fails. I know He did with me providing life after my first love.

CATCHING THE BIG FISH

I got into fishing pretty heavy and bought a bass boat with a big motor to get to where I wanted to go in a hurry. Never really figured out why I needed to get there in such a hurry. The boat had two fishing chairs that were top-of-the-line. I had fishing graphs that looked down and to the side. A fish couldn't hide from me. Twelve rods and reels and five tackle boxes were close by. I was a bona fide fisherman.

Today I would be fishing for strippers in the Congaree River. I casted off and anchored on the low side of a sandbar. Now, I would sit back and wait on the fish.

I noticed a young boy coming out on the sandbar. He had one rod and reel and a can that he carried his extra lead and hooks in. He had to fix the reel on the rod before he got started fishing. Finally, he baited the hook and threw out toward my line, but well short of reaching my line. After a while he hooked something, and the fight was on. It lasted a good thirty minutes, and finally this large stripper was pulled in. The boy was excited. He kept saying, "I wonder what he weighs." Now being a bona fide fisherman, I happened to have one of the digital scales. Pulling up my reels and anchor, I headed to the shore. The fish weighed thirty-two pounds. By the way, I didn't catch a thing.

Alyssa, I had everything I needed to catch that fish. All he had was a rod and reel and a gallon can, but he caught the fish.

In the ministry, I have seen parents give their kids everything they wanted; as they grew up, it continued. They went to college, and yet they were worthless. I have seen family businesses go belly up when these kids got involved. They had everything for success but failed.

Then I have seen kids growing up in poverty and become a success. They worked hard, and they made it. It's not what they had but what they believed. We hear people say, "Where there is a will, there is a way," and I have seen that. Alyssa, believe in yourself and take the gift God has given you and use it. The sky is the limit with God involved, and you will catch the big fish.

PLANTING NEW TREES

When I was eight or nine, the timber was cut on the homeplace. I remember them setting up the sawmill on the upper property. That was so amazing.

After it was set up, they brought in two Belgium gray draft horses to pull the logs to the mill. Now we had no television, so I had never seen a horse this size. They were giants to this young boy. Those horses were so strong, and they would work all day. At evening the handlers would feed them hay and grain under a makeshift shed. Next day they were again ready to work.

The second time the timber was cut was when I was in the Air Force. They used saws to cut and a skipjack to pull out the logs to be loaded on trucks.

The third cutting, I sold the timber, and they came with a tree harvester that took the whole tree down. A timberjack would take a group of logs, stacked by the harvester to the loading prep and loaded on trucks. The trees were cleared out, all wood salvaged.

The following fall, a team of Mexicans came in and sprayed the brush and new growth. It killed everything. The next fall, planting would take place after the fourth frost.

So on February 5, 2018, a team of Mexicans arrived to plant the pine trees. It took a team of twelve and four hours to plant eighteen acres. Using a machete-like tool, they would throw it into the ground. This would open a hole for the tree to be planted. These guys were good!

Alyssa, these trees are for you. You will see them mature, and you and your mom will have them harvested. Always try to do something for the future—if not for you, for someone else. Make the world a little better for all. Planting trees is just a small way to make God's world better.

MY COWBOY DAYS

I was fishing at a neighbor's pond when his wife came riding up on her horse. We talked for a while, and she asked me if I had ever ridden a horse. I was thirteen, and riding a horse was something I had never done. I told her no. "Would you like to try riding?" she asked. I was somewhat hesitant, but she said her horse couldn't run and that he would be the perfect horse for me to ride the first time. I agreed to try it.

Getting into the saddle, there was a problem. Her legs were longer than mine, and so one foot was in the stirrup and the other was out. She said, "Don't worry, he will walk across the pond dam to the gate on the other side." She walked behind me, and all of a sudden, this horse took off running toward the gate. I tried to stop her, but no use. I called her some choice names, which I asked God later to forgive me.

The gate was coming up, and I thought, *This crazy thing is going to jump it.* I was wrong, she didn't jump, but dug his hooves in, and I kept going across the gate.

I jumped the gate, battered and bruised; I got up to face her owner asking why I made her run. "She never did that before," she added. I told her, "I didn't kick, hit, or even say giddy up to this horse. She just took off."

My next encounter was some weeks later on that same pond dam. The husband was riding his horse and stopped to talk. He told me his wife told him that I had gotten thrown by old Princess. He told me what I needed to do was get back on a horse. He then told me about old Gentle Giant. "Now here is a horse you can ride," he insisted. I had healed from the first ride, so I agreed to ride again—same pond dam, different horse.

It started out good just walking along, even the stirrups fit my feet. This was going to be great. About halfway across the dam, trouble, he took a flying leap into the pond. I hit the water coming up with the frog lilies all over me. Again, those words, "He never did that before."

My last ride came some months later at a birthday party. A pony was being ridden by all the little children. They pulled his tail and mane, and he just let them do it. The owner asked me if I had ever ridden horses, and I said, "Yes, but I had been thrown both times." He talked about little Jake and what a great disposition he had. "Look at him with the children. You need to ride Jake to give you a good experience." Stupid me said, "Okay."

When I got on his back, little Jake turned and looked at me and then ran under a limb knocking me off. Again the words, "He never did that before."

My cowboy days are over. I will never get on another horse on this side of eternity. I tried three times, and I struck out. Alyssa, I am glad you can ride, I admire you, but I will never have the love you have for horses. You keep riding, dear, and I'll stand off to the side proud of you. My cowboy days are over.

Matthew Rucker

MOONSHINE

My family never made moonshine, but neighbors did, and they used the springs close to us. A chief moonshiner was who I'll call Sman. He was a neighbor close to our family. Now all this occurred when I was ten to thirteen years old in my life.

Now the sheriff of the county was my Uncle Elliott. The sheriff's department was always looking for stills. I loved my uncle, but I was on the side of Sman. You see, we knew where the still was because of always being in the woods, so it was like having a secret. On one occasion we were posted on the county road while Sman was running a run of moonshine. We had a fifty-five-gallon drum and a big stick. If law enforcement showed up, we beat the drum. Uncle Elliott drives up, and we are beating the drum. "What are you boys doing?" he asked. "Playing cowboys and Indians, and we are the Indians," I replied. "Well, be careful," he said as he drove off.

Sman would rotate using the springs to make moonshine. My grandmother would see him as he would go to the still before dark. One evening she was frying fish and told me to take Sman fish and bread. Going to the still was no problem because it was almost in the backyard. This was something that

Granny would do for Sman, and he seemed to make sure she knew where he was.

Now when I would go to the still location, my beagle dog Sooner would run ahead. Sooner would run into the still area, and Sman would answer, "That you, Matt?" I would answer, "Yes, sir," as I brought his food to him.

Alyssa, I've sat in the still and helped Sman mix everything up to run moonshine. I've handed buckets to him while he ran a run. I've watched him cut it to the right alcohol level so that it is drinkable. Most of this was done at night, and that to a young boy was exciting. My parents loved Sman and trusted him, and I still love Sman today.

We made strong friends from people outside our family, even someone like Sman. Try to make friends with all people because you're no better than they are. Never put yourself above anyone. Learn to love everybody. Sman is my friend, almost ninety-five now, and I saw him just the other day at a friend's house. He had brought my friend some turnips in a bag. Sman reminded him to set it down easy, for also in the bag was a quart of moonshine.

MAKING THE SHOT

It was Friday night and time to coon hunt with Mr. Petty, Mr. Tillis, and Mr. Cotton. We loaded up the dogs, and to the swamp, we headed. It was a real windy night to hunt the raccoon. After a while the dogs picked up a trail and finally treed the raccoon, way up in the top of the tree. He was in the upper small branches of the tall tree and blown in all directions by the wind.

Normally we would take the rifle and shoot the coon, but Mr. Petty and Mr. Tillis had taken up shooting a pistol. They began trying to shoot the coon but had no luck. Mr. Cotton, who had been drinking, said, "Give me the pistol, I can knock him out." Mr. Tillis told him he couldn't hit the side of a barn because he was too drunk. Mr. Cotton kept on asking, and Mr. Tillis said, "Here is one bullet, you get one shot, then sit down and shut up." Now Mr. Tillis and Mr. Petty had shot many times standing and even lay on the ground and shot. Mr. Cotton takes the pistol and, weaving back and forth in sync with the moving limbs, fired. Down came the coon. "I got him, Tillis," he said. Mr. Tillis answered, "Yeah, a lucky shot."

About an hour later we treed again, and the same situation—tall tree, wind blowing, coon in the top of the tree. Mr. Petty and Mr. Tillis start shooting, but no luck. To shut Mr. Cotton up again, they gave him one shot, and lo and behold, down comes the coon.

Alyssa, that was one hard shot to make, but to do it twice is unbelievable. He made both shots. Now that's hard to do, but I think something even harder is trying to get someone to turn their life around and to turn their life from bad to good. How hard God works at turning a person around. He had to work hard with me to make the shot. I fought him because I wanted to be free to do as I pleased. Little did I know that the very thing I wanted to be free, he gave to me. Instead of being tossed here and there in the winds of the world, He put me on the straight and narrow. Now that I think of it, I think it was easier to make that shot on the raccoon that night than bringing me home to Christ.

Matthew Rucker

"NANNY"

om was the most loving, giving, nonjudgmental, and pillar of strength that I have known. I loved her dearly and still love her.

She worked in a sewing room for little pay. Yet she helped provide for the family. When I got my first new car, my mom cosigned with me, making the payments for me. She always supported me and encouraged me and pointed out to me when I was wrong. When I went into the ministry, she was my biggest fan.

Mom would always help people in trouble or crisis. If there was a death, or some sickness, she would show up with food and always a cake. Black or white, it didn't matter, she never saw color.

When her health began to fail, she had this strong faith that she and God could handle it, and never complained, just a positive attitude. She was an inspiration to the community, and everyone called her Nanny.

She loved her family, friends, and neighbors. Living alone and losing her sight, her spirit never sank. She would let you know, "I'm blind but not handicapped." It was so interesting that Mom every day had someone bring food to her home. God was returning the blessings to her as she had done for people. Every day was an adventure with her and her little dog Sandy.

Sandy became her eyes and ears and protector. Mom lived each day to its fullest.

She finally decided to go to a nursing home. The staff loved her. We had to bring for the staff different kinds of snacks, which she gave out freely. When they had problems, guess who was there.

She had several roommates. The staff asked if this certain lady who got along with no one could move in her room. Mother took her in and changed the lady to a different person. Mother's attitude and spirit was contagious, and Margaret changed. When Mom died, Margaret said, "I lost my best friend."

Mom's death was quiet and peaceful. She told us that she wouldn't reach her ninetieth birthday. She died four hours before her birthday. I still miss her so.

Alyssa, this was your great-grandmother, and she loved you. Remember you come from good genes. I see some of Mother in you. Your giving spirit, your grin, your independent spirit, and your love—these are all characteristics of your great-grandmother. Be proud of your heritage. Who knows, keep it up, and one day when you are older, the community might call you Nanny.

MY MILITARY SERVICE

I am proud of my military service—serving twelve years in the Air Force and National Guard. In the Air Force, I was in Top Secret Nuclear Missiles; my missile was called the Hound Dog—fifty-eight feet long, with a jet engine under it to propel it.

My job was to program it and to fix it if it broke. This missile was mounted between the engines under both wings of the B52. As we would say, there are two birds under the wings of the big bird. These missiles were heavily guarded by soldiers and security dogs, and I made friends with all the dogs.

Flight days were Tuesday and Thursday. If the missile missed the target by one thousand feet, it was a bad flight, and they expected me to repair the problem when we got back to the hangar. I am still filled with pride when I watch that old bomber take off.

Now in the National Guard, I worked with tanks. Do you know that a tank has to dig in before it is fired, and you can see the projectile when it leaves the barrel? The range on the tank was twelve miles, and my job was a portable radar unit that they used to help line up the target.

I remember on one occasion we were standing in the observation site, and the call was made to fire twelve miles up range. We heard the projectile coming, and it was coming toward us. We dove behind a little hill about the time the projectile hit and exploded. It knocked the shed down that we had been standing under. I learned a lot of new curse words when that colonel called up range to speak to the individuals that had set up shot.

The military will always be special to me, they are my brothers and sisters. I appreciate each and every one of them, and I would ask of you, Alyssa, to say a special prayer each night for them and their service.

KNOCKED DOWN IN THE NIGHT

It was 2:00 a.m., and I was driving home from the air base Seymour Johnson. I had driven for about an hour, and I had to use the bathroom. It was one of those long asphalt roads, the perfect place to stop. I pulled my Volkswagen beetle off on the side of the road. It was a dark night with light rain as I went down off the road. I was relieving myself watching the road, and it was just a quiet place in the country.

All of a sudden it felt like the lower half of my body exploded, and I hit the ground. I thought to myself, *I must be shot.* My legs didn't want to work, and I just hurt. Thinking to myself, *If I had been shot, I would have heard it.* I crawled up to the Volkswagen still thinking what really had happened to me. Reaching the car, I pulled myself up with legs like Jell-O. I finally checked for blood—none.

I got a flashlight to investigate what had happened. Walking back to the scene of the crime, I saw it. There was an electric fence, and urine is salty and makes a great conductor for electricity. To this day, I don't know if I finished or not.

Alyssa, things in life can happen this fast. The death of a friend in a wreck or shooting, an overdose, or heart attack can come without warning and blindside you. It was easy for me to figure my situation out, but others leave you asking why. You won't get all the answers in this life. You will ask why, but the answers won't come. It's okay to ask why, but sometimes all you can do is trust God, who knows why. In the meantime, it will hurt you, like peeing on an electric fence.

MY CALL TO THE MINISTRY

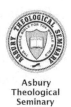

Asbury
Theological
Seminary

First of all, let me explain what a call from God is. When God quietly works in one's life to move them in a certain direction, He never forces but opens doors for the path He wants you to take.

My call was a process over five years. It began in 1971 when I was asked to preach one night in a youth revival by my home pastor. I was in the Air Force and didn't have time to do this, so I kept putting him off. He kept on until I finally said yes to shut him up. I preached on a Saturday night, and little did I know that the feeling that night would haunt me for the next five years.

I became a lay speaker in the Methodist Church hoping that would curb the feeling, it didn't. I kept going to college, but something was missing.

Finally in April of 1976, it all came to a head. My girlfriend had just left me, and I was down. I went to see a missionary friend of mine who was home on furlough. I told her my story, and she said, "Let me read you one verse." She read, "Seek ye first he kingdom of God and all these things will be added unto you." I didn't hear a voice or see a bright light, but I knew God showed up. I felt his presence, and I knew what I was going to do. I was heading to the ministry.

Now the seminary I wanted to attend was Asbury in Wilmore, Kentucky. But there was a waiting list to get in, and I would have to do all the testing before being accepted. I went to the school for the test, and they told me that because I tested late and because of the waiting list, I should look to the following year to enter. Nevertheless, I had this pushing for me to go to seminary, so I loaded my Volkswagen and set out on faith, with no confirmation of acceptance to Asbury.

I arrived and stood in line without any papers that had to be presented to the registrar. Yet I had this calm feeling and kept moving forward. It was my turn, and he asked for my papers, and at that moment, a man walked up to him and handed him some papers. He looked at them and said, "Matthew Rucker." I answered, "Yes." It was my papers of acceptance. While I was at seminary, I looked for that man on campus to thank him, but I never saw him again. I will always believe he was an angel, because when I asked about him to the staff, they knew nothing.

Alyssa, faith has always driven me just as it did then. My faith has continued to increase through my journey in this life. What is faith? Well, I think of it this way: go as far as you know then take another step. That's faith. Going beyond all you know to the unknown, and God enters there. My faith is the most important thing in my life, and I believe God's word. I believe His promises, and I believe He has his hand on my life, and I will see Him one day.

So, Alyssa, when you hear "PeePaw is dead," don't you believe it. At that moment, I shall be more alive than I have ever been when He calls me home.

Matthew Rucker

PADDLING YOUR RIVER

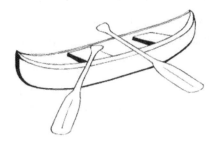

It was spring break at seminary. We were getting ready to graduate, so we wanted to do something fun. One of our classmates suggested we go home with him and canoe down the river. Five of us agreed to go, so we headed to Alabama. His dad provided us with two canoes, and his mom provided sandwiches and drinks for lunch. Gathered at the river, we were ready to cast off.

I was in the first canoe in front to paddle. Peter was in the middle, and Larry (from Alabama) in the rear, also a paddler. The second canoe had two Lumbee Indians as paddlers, with Hugh in the middle. Now Hugh had bought an expensive felt hat with a wide brim. It was to protect his head from the sun. He looked like somebody out of the Old West.

We cast off first and around the bend we went. We lost sight of the other canoe. It was running behind us. Larry had picked a place on the river to stop for lunch, a sandbar. This was an all-day trip, and this location was about halfway. We landed and waited on the other crew.

We see them finally as they come around the bend and watch them hit the bank on the other side. Struggling they came out of the brush on the side of the river. They went a short distance and into the other side of the river fighting the brush again.

They finally land on the sandbar. Hugh gets out of the canoe and wringing his shirt out. He looks at his Lumbee friends and says, "I have lost all faith in the ability of the American Indian. You boys ought to have canoeing in your blood, but you have just about drowned me." They had let him down.

Alyssa, people will let you down, your mom and dad, grandparents, sister and brothers, and friends. You will let people down as well. Nobody is perfect. That's why we need forgiveness. Alyssa, when someone lets you down, you will have to decide whether to forgive or distance yourself. I have learned that there is only one who won't let me down, and that is Jesus Christ. He is the same today as He was yesterday—always steady, wanting the best for you. Put your faith in Christ, not people, for they will let you down. Christ will help you paddle your river of life. Enjoy the ride.

RACHAEL'S BIRTH

Rachael was our firstborn. There is always great excitement with the first. It had been a hard pregnancy, and besides that, our insurance wouldn't pay for it. The payment for the pregnancy was donated by my seminary professor's son-in-law. Now that was an answered prayer.

Time went by so fast, and soon we had to head to the hospital. Bags had been packed, and we were ready to go. When your mom's water broke, we hit the road to Lexington Medical Center in Kentucky.

Everything was made ready for Rachael's arrival. Things were going along fine, and the doctor came in. He told us something was going wrong with the baby's heartbeat, and if it didn't improve, he would have to take the baby. I remember watching the monitor for any sign. All at once the doctor and the nurse came in. "We've got to take the baby now," he said. With that they wheeled your MeeMaw out of the room. The nurse took me to a small waiting room. I sat there by myself. That was the longest and most anxious time in my life. I prayed they both would be okay. I begged God to please answer my prayer. After what seemed to be eternity, they came in and said everything was okay, but the baby would have to go to the intensive care unit.

Alyssa, this was a scary time in my life not knowing if I were going to lose your mom that day. I tuned to the only source I knew who could help, God. Always remember when you get into one of those hard places in life and you don't know where to turn, turn to God. Believe He wants the best for you. Trust him when it may seem impossible. Cling to Him when you are scared, and pray. Everything will be all right.

KEEPING PRIORITIES STRAIGHT

Uncle Charlie loved to fish. One day we had to fix the fence because the pigs were getting out on the highway. Those pigs were to be sold for money for the family or to be butchered for meat. I was helping him to secure them. While getting ready to dig a hole for a post, I raked back some leaves to dig and discovered some worms. Seeing them, Uncle Charlie shouted, "Get a can, son." We gathered them up, and off to the house we headed. We grabbed some fishing poles and got in the truck, and to Wolfe Lake we headed. The pigs were no longer a necessity, fishing was. Fishing was the number one important item.

Alyssa, you have to keep your priorities straight in life. There are things that are priorities and things that are not. Food, shelter, transportation, gas, clothes, and insurance are real priorities of life. Fishing is not, it's a hobby. I remember when I wanted to buy a boat, but I waited five years to buy it. Oh, I could have bought it, but I would have put a strain on the family financially. I had to wait. When you push a hobby before necessities, you will always end up short in money. Something will have to suffer. You will either go deeper in debt or turn to family members to help out. Many times putting them in difficulty, struggling to make ends meet. Making a hobby a priority when you can't afford it will put you in the poor house real quick.

Yes, Uncle Charlie lost some of his pigs on the road to letting the fence go. It took money out of his pocket all because fishing was more important than things really needed. There will always be worms under the leaves waiting for you. Alyssa, keep the stress away and just fix the fence. Take care of your priorities first and keep a hobby in its place.

WATCHING GOD TAKE PICTURES

I have always been fascinated with lightning. I guess it all started when I was young, and while sitting under a shed, I saw lightning strike a tree in the yard. The streaks of the fire coming down the tree were awesome. The sound was deafening. There began my love for lightning.

In later years with the kids, Rachael and Brandon, I introduced them to lightning. I would take them out into the carport and sit in the boat when a thunderstorm was in the area. We would wait for the storm to come close. I told the kids that God was taking pictures. Lightning would flash, and they would say, "God took another picture." Their mom thought it was stupid, but we enjoyed it so.

Alyssa, those were precious memories sitting in that boat. I was a kid again sitting under that shed waiting to see the awesome power of lightning. To me it represents only a small portion of the power of God. The power that's available to you and me. He is an awesome God and an all-powerful God. Watch the lightning strike, hear the thunder roll, and remember, it's only God taking pictures.

THE CAT'S BIG SENDOFF

The kids wanted a pet, so a church member gave them both a cat. They grew into two fine tomcats. Finally of age, they were ready for surgery. They were both neutered and brought back home. We kept them in the garage overnight. The next morning we let them out, and one of the cats ran up on the highway and was killed by a car. I don't think he could handle neutering psychologically, so he committed suicide.

The kids insisted we have a funeral for the dead cat, so we planned a funeral. We dug a grave and gathered flowers from the field. We gathered around the grave, and I read some scripture, had a prayer, and said some words about the cat. The service concluded with the three of us singing "Jesus Loves Me." We then placed the flowers on the grave after we covered it up.

Alyssa, this was some sendoff for this cat, but it was important to your mom and Uncle Brandon. They felt better after the service, so good that we loaded up to go get pizza. Remember, animals are important to Jesus too. Remember how he cared for the little sparrows. But I can't help but wonder how he felt with this cat's burial. I think he smiled as he looked down and said, "Now that cat had a big sendoff."

THE ANGEL'S VISIT

I t was the time of the fall revival at my small country church. I asked a friend of mine to speak each night at the four-day event. It was the first night, and Rev. P. and I left to go up to get there early. Arriving at the church, we met Mr. J.; he had come early to light the heaters.

He shared with us a story of how after lighting the heaters he went to the altar to pray for the revival, and while praying, he heard the front door open. Pausing he looked around and saw two people dressed in white. He said he finished his prayer to get up to greet what he thought were early arrivers. "When I got up and looked around, they were gone," he said. I went outside thinking they were on the porch, but no one, not even a car. He told us, "I believe these were angels coming to bless the revival," he said.

The service began, and it came time for Rev. P. to speak. He said, "Before I speak, I wonder if Mr. J. would share that story he shared earlier with Matt and I."

Mr. J. told the story up to the point of "I believe those were angels," and two girls at the back of the church said, "That was us, Uncle J." Mr. J. replied, "No such thing, they had white on." They replied, pointing to their dresses, "These are almost white." Mr. J. replied, "Well, where were you when

I went outside?" "We were in the bathroom (bathrooms were outside back of the church), we heard you go by," one of the girls responded. "No, those were angels, and I know they were," Mr. J. responded.

Rev. P. just stood there as this conversation took place that never got settled.

Alyssa, I believe in angels. Elvis Pressley had a song about looking like an angel but was the devil in disguise. Not everyone you meet is an angel. They may act like it, but be careful. They will tell you what you want to hear, promise you the world, but look out. Learn to lead with your head and not your heart. Keep a strong faith, and the real angels will stand up.

A CALM IN THE MIDST OF THE STORM

It was one of those summer days hot and humid. I took my daughter and son to the lake, Lake Russell. This is a wooded lake with no houses. We unloaded the boat and set off down the lake to fish. Everything was going great.

One of the great threats on the lake in summer are thunderstorms. You don't want to be on the water when one blows up. I noticed some clouds, but we were in a cove hidden from the big picture. All of a sudden we heard thunder. We had to get back to the landing and the truck. When I pulled out, the cove the storm was all around us, and I couldn't go across the big water.

Returning to the cove, we had to get off the lake. Lightning was flashing all around us. We got out the boat and moved away from the water under some small trees. I had a piece of canvas to cover, and we all huddled on the ground under the canvas. Both kids were scared, and I tried to be brave. It seemed the storm would never end, but eventually it did. We got in the boat and headed up the lake to the dock.

Alyssa, your mom still remembers this day as well as I. Storms still come on the lakes, and they are dangerous, but storms also occur on dry land as well. Think of a family going through a divorce. Now that's a storm and brings lots of fear. Your mom and Uncle Brandon were afraid during the divorce and hid under anger and fear. I tried to protect them the best I could, but it leaves lasting memories.

Alyssa, you will face storms in your life. It may be a breakup with a sweetheart, death of a family member, the death of your horse, or some illness. You are safe in the cove right now, but you can't see the big picture of what is on the horizon. Yes, storms will come, but always remember God will always provide calmness in the midst of the storm. Wrap yourself in His love and hang on till the storm passes.

SENDING "JOHN" HOME

My first ministerial appointment was to three churches, and one of these churches was a rural church. Several of the members had those old Southern homes, large homes with great front columns.

About eight weeks into my appointment, I was asked by a church member to speak with her after the service. I met with her, and she told me about her house being haunted by a ghost. This ghost was a Confederate soldier who had been killed in her house. His name was John. Now she wanted me to come and remove him from the house. Now I have learned you never laugh at anything people share with you, so I agreed to go over to her house next week on Tuesday night.

Now I had been taught many things at seminary, but removing a ghost wasn't one of them. I looked through various books, but no luck. Tuesday arrives, and I go over to her house about sundown. We had some coffee, and I asked when John usually showed up. "You'll know," she said, "you'll know." In a little while, I hear what sounds like someone moving silverware—spoons, forks, and knives. She looks at me and says, "That's John, and he'll open the door pretty soon," and sure enough, the door opened. Now my mind is screaming *RUN!*, but I sat there. The door closes, and then there were sounds like someone moaning, chains, and someone walking, and other noises. She was used to John, but I was just meeting him.

"Well, what are you going to do?" she asked me. I called out to John and told him he needed to go to heaven where he would be happy. I told him he was frightening Mrs. Smith and the house was too small for both of them. "It is okay, you can leave, John, it is okay," I added.

The house got deathly quiet, and soon after, I left. I had never had that kind of situation, and sleep didn't come that night. I heard all kind of noises in my mind. I was afraid John had come home with me.

Next Sunday, Mrs. Smith reported to me that John had left, no noises, and that she might have a friend whose house may be haunted. I suggested, "It probably wasn't, but just pray for your friend." I sure didn't want to go through evicting another ghost.

MY LAST SNOW SKIING

The church bus was loaded, and to the mountains we headed. A weekend of snow skiing. I had never been on snow skis, but I knew how to water-ski, so how hard could it be? There were experts on the bus, people who had skied before. I found out some of those experts lied when we hit the slopes.

We stopped and rented skis, and up the mountain we went. By the time we hit the slope, night had fallen. I headed for the beginners slope. Now they have a rope you grab a hold of that pulls you up the hill to the top of the beginners slope. I was in line with other kids. As I grabbed a hold of the rope, following the little kids, I fell down. While they stood up, it dragged me up the little hill. At the top I tried to get up, and some helpful man—tired of my struggling—helped me to my feet. After a few trips, I was feeling pretty good, and no, it's nothing like water-skiing.

Yes, I was ready for the intermediate level slope. I managed to remain standing up the slope, and my confidence soared, I was ready. I got into position, and I was ready to attack this course. Off I went, my speed increasing, and about middleways, a mother and child step out onto the course. I hadn't quite mastered stopping or trying to turn. Now, remind you, it's dark, but I chose to go around them. I chose to go behind them, and lo and behold, I went airborne. I had graduated to ski jumping. It was a cliff of about twenty feet, and I fell to the bottom. Making a quick check, I didn't think I broke anything except the ski pole. It was in a perfect ninety degrees. About that time, the little boy came over to the edge and said, "That was some cool fall, mister."

If I could have just reached the top, I would have shown him what cool was. But you see, they had automatic snowmakers on earlier, and down where I landed was covered with ice. One of the helpers got a rope, and again I was dragged up the cliff.

When I turned in my skis and the attendant asked what happened, I told her she didn't want to know. I told her that it involved a mother and child stepping out causing me to go over the cliff. I also told her if I could have made it back on the slope, there might have been a murder. I had to ask God to forgive me of that.

Alyssa, a man or woman has to know his/her limitations. You see, just when I thought I would be the next great skier, I went over the cliff. Make sure you know what you're doing before you do it. That was one of longest falls in my life because in my head were all those cliffs that I saw from the bus ride up. Thank God I was well padded because of the cold. But see, it was my macho attitude of "I've got this" that got me into trouble. Take time and learn before you try. If I had done that, maybe that wouldn't have been my first and last snow ski trip.

ROLLING-SKATING FIRST AND LAST TIME

It was your mom's birthday, and she wanted to have a roller-skating party. We got a cake, drinks, and ice cream; and all the little darlings gathered at the rink. The kids got their skates, mothers got their skates, and even the two dads skated up. I was left guarding the refreshments.

Rachael, your mom, kept asking me to skate. I was the only one at this party who wasn't on wheels. So old stupid me says, "How hard can it be? I can do this."

I rented the skates and put them on. It was easy while I was on the rug, but now to the rink. There was a railing around the rink, and I moved toward it. Little kids were just zooming around the rink, making it look so easy. Taking a deep breath, I stepped onto the rink and nearly wrenched my shoulder out as I went down.

Rachael and her friends kept encouraging me, and I did form a pattern: three steps forward and then hit the floor. I never realized how far it is around the wall of a rink, and afraid to let go, I struggled on. The end was in sight, glad to get back where I started. I remember thinking, *I will not get on these things again.*

Now everybody had gotten off the rink enjoying drinks, ice cream, and cake; and I was coming in for landing. I hit the rail as my skates hit the carpet, and down I went taking out the table and knocking over mothers and children. Those moms turned into mama bears and gave me a severe tongue-lashing. Some even left and went home. I tried to explain, but it fell on deaf ears. Taking my skates off, I never put on a set again.

Alyssa, I could hardly walk the next day because I was so sore. I didn't mean to spoil the party, but I did. I don't think I even gained the trust of some of those mothers no matter how many times I apologized. I spoiled the party with skates, but you can spoil a party or some good occasion with your attitude. A bad attitude can destroy fun and a good time. Always watch your attitude; it can break up a party so quickly. A bad attitude is like being on a runaway horse. You will get where you don't want to go, like when I roller-skated the first and last time. Keep a positive attitude, and make God and me proud.

Matthew Rucker

THE NIGHT I DIED

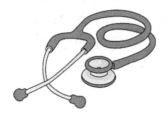

I t was a Sunday night when the pain in my stomach began. It continued to get worse, and I called my doctor. He had an office at the hospital, so he told me to meet him there. Arriving, I went to his room, and he was waiting. He listened to me, and with pain so great, he gave me a shot of morphine. I had never received morphine before, and it knocked me out. The last thing I remember was being in Doc's office.

Sometime later I woke up in a strange room trying to figure out where I was. A nurse came in to take my vitals, and I just watched her; taking my left arm, she checked for a pulse. She kept moving her finger and then screamed, "Code blue." Within a few minutes, the room filled with people. The doctor came in, ripped open my shirt, and placed the stethoscope to my chest. "I've got a pulse," he said. He looked at me and said, "We almost lost you, but everything is fine now," he added. I asked what happened, and he explained that the nurse couldn't find a pulse in my arm. I told him that it was hard to find one in my left arm. He told the nurse she needed to add that to the chart. They all left.

By myself again, I began to think about what had happened. I thought if I had died, it was a piece of cake—no fear at all for me.

Alyssa, I don't think death will be that bad. I think it is as being put under anesthesia. You try to fight it, but you drift away and later wake up in a new place. Gradually everything becomes clear. Death to me is the anesthesia that God gives us when we change bodies. It's going to be okay, kind of like the night I died in the hospital room.

WHOSE FUNERAL IS IT?

It was my first funeral: a dear little lady, Mary. I had only been at the church for a month, and the family knew I didn't really know her. They suggested that the former pastor come back and I could assist him. Boy, did I feel a sense of relief.

We talked on the phone, and he said if I would read some scripture and have a prayer, he would handle the rest. He asked if this was my first funeral, and I said, "Yes." He responded, "Well, why don't you use this as a time to learn?"

He showed up, three-piece suit and a pocket handkerchief. I got up and read the scripture and then prayed. Next was a hymn, and then he was up.

He looked out across the congregation and finally said, "We are here today to remember Martha." Now I'm thinking, I thought her name was Mary. Maybe it was Mary Martha, so I let it go.

He talked on of going to her house and always having a biscuit that Myrtle had made. "Myrtle, who the heck is Myrtle?" And by the looks on the family's faces, they were wondering too. But I'm here to learn, so I let it go.

He then told some stories and then finished by saying, "Maude is gone, but we will never forget her." Now I am really confused, and the dear family—they are looking at each other just as confused. Nevertheless, we all stood and sang "Amazing Grace."

He and I led the pallbearers and the casket out of the chapel, followed by the family out the church. He was going to ride with me to the graveside, so he got in my car. I couldn't help but ask him what this dear lady's name was. He looked at me like I was an idiot and said, "Mary." I told him, "I was confused because you never used her real name. You called her Martha, Myrtle, and Maude, but never Mary." He looked at his watch and said, "Oh my, look at the time, I have a meeting that I have to get to. You handle the graveside, and please explain to the family." He then got out of my car.

We arrived at the graveside, and I did the committal, and I said, "We lay Mary to rest today." Everyone gave a sigh of relief knowing whose funeral it was.

Alyssa, the older you get, the more you have to write things down. I have to now more than ever, even people's names. Nothing wrong with having notes in life, they can help you. Always be prepared in whatever you do. Flying by the set of your pants can cause you to crash and burn.

Matthew Rucker

MAMA COMES HOME

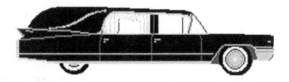

My first appointment to a church, in the Pee Dee, introduced me to the customs of this area of the state with funerals. In this area they would bring the deceased home the day before the funeral. Such was the case with Mrs. Jones.

She had ten children—one boy and nine girls, and they asked me to be at the home when Mama came home for the last time. She would arrive at 10:00 a.m. on the day before the funeral. I arrived at 9:30 a.m. and waited with the family.

She lived in an old farmhouse with a long driveway coming off a dirt road. We all gathered in the living room that had one of those large windows facing the driveway.

Finally, we see the hearse as it comes down the dirt road turning into the driveway. We were in a group hug with the girls crying and saying, "Mama's coming home for the last time, Mama's coming home for the last time."

I was facing the window, and I watched as the hearse pulled into the yard and then backed up into the carport. The son had gone out into the carport to meet them. But then I see the hearse pull out and head back down the driveway. I thought to myself, *Surely they didn't leave her in the carport.* About that time, the son came in. "Where is Mama?" they asked. He responded, "They forgot Mama." And they truly did.

They returned with Mama, and we got her into the house. The family moved her favorite chair and placed the casket in its place. Also, a table was placed at the head and foot of the casket. The first table had cakes, pies, and cookies; and the second table had drinks. It was almost as if they were saying, "Have a piece of pie, visit with Mama, and make sure you get your drink." I have never or since then seen such a setup for a visitation.

I had the opportunity to talk with both the funeral home guys later, and they said each thought the other had loaded her (Mama).

Alyssa, this is a time of sadness, and right in the middle is humor. There is humor in all situations. Always look for the humor, and you will find it. Learn to laugh; I know I have, especially when they forgot Mama.

BREAKING THE ICE FOR JESUS

A family of six came to me after church and said they wanted to be baptized. They also informed me that they wanted to do it in a mountain stream they loved. It was in the middle of January in the mountains, so I'm thinking of spring time for this event. "When are you looking at doing it?" I asked. "How about next Saturday?" the father responded. *Next Saturday,* I thought, *what about the weather?* "That's a special day for us," they said, "the weather will be fine."

As Saturday approaches, I watched the weather. They are calling for snow showers and temperature in the teens. I checked with them, and they were excited about the occasion.

Saturday morning, I met them at the church, and we set out with snow on the ground. We finally arrived, and the stream that they chose was—according to the sign—three miles away. *Three miles away,* I thought, *in this weather.* And so we started out walking, and I grew to hate those little signs that marked the distance. Only two and half miles, only two miles, only one and half miles, etc., and the colder I became. We finally arrived at the pool with ice everywhere. I broke the ice on the small pool. I baptized all six of them with ice water. After the service, my fingers and toes were numb. They were so grateful yet freezing, and now the walk back—oh, happy day. I could have kissed my truck when I saw it.

The next Sunday, they reported to the church what a wonderful experience it was. I remember thinking, *Was I at the wrong place?*

Alyssa, sometimes people have special days they want things done. Nothing will stop them. No matter if rain, sleet, or snow is falling. They will put up with a lot to make it happen. Yes, I was cold and my feet wet, but to make them happy, I would break the ice for Jesus.

MY DIVORCE

I thought things were going fine in our marriage, but my wife didn't think so. Things came to a head when I agreed to let a church member's daughter stay with us. Her father had kicked her out, and I suggested that she could stay with us. Things were okay for a while, but a change was taking place. Soon my wife began talking of us separating, and I agreed to get a place in the neighboring town while I pursued a chaplaincy program. My first day at the hospital, I was served divorce papers, which came as a total shock.

Now I didn't want a divorce and tried to talk it out with her, but I was kicking a dead dog. I kept fighting it because of the kids. I didn't want your mom and your uncle Brandon to go through a divorce. This was a time of hell for me. No matter what I did, the day finally came, and I was in a courtroom before a judge. I left a divorced man, a hurting man, and an angry man.

Thinking of the future, I couldn't see myself as a minister. I was damaged goods, feeling dirty. How could I go on with the kids not around? I missed them so.

I then realized I had to go on. The hardest part was forgiving my ex-wife. Yet I endured and found out that there is life after divorce, and I ended up with the greatest love of my life.

Alyssa, you don't remember any of this, but one day you may face the same pain. I hope not. But if you do remember, you can't make a person love you. No matter what you do or promise, they feel happiness is elsewhere. Sometimes even if you love that person, you have to let go. Yes, it is hard, very hard, but you can't change them. You pick yourself up and move on, just like I did in my divorce.

BULLY COMES HOME

My wife and I gave her mom a bull for her herd. His name was Bully. After several months, Bully went missing. It seemed that he had just vanished. I had to go to Annual Conference in Spartanburg and planned to stay at my mother-in-law's house. Annual Conference is a yearly meeting of South Carolina Methodist ministers. I would also look for Bully.

My mother-in-law called me the night before I left to go up for conference and said she had found Bully. He was at a neighbor's farm in a pasture of cows. She and I went over after I arrived to see if it was Bully. When we drove up, I could see it was him.

I walked out into the pasture up to him and looked at him. I finally spoke to him saying, "What are you doing over here? You need to get back home, you know better than this. Lord, convince him to go home."

The next day, I wanted to check the fence to see if I could find where he got out. I was down in the bottom by the creek when my phone rang. It was my brother-in-law, and he said, "Guess who I'm looking at?" I replied, "Who?" He responded, "Bully," and I told him, "Don't kid about this." He said, "No, I'm looking at him now." I got in the golf cart and headed up to the upper pasture, and there was Bully.

Now, I hadn't found anyplace where he could have gotten out. The neighbor checked his fence, and no place was found where the fence was down. To this day, I don't know how he got out or how he got back in.

Alyssa, the Bible says, "God works in mysterious ways His wonders to perform." I prayed that He would send Bully home, and I believe He did. Don't be afraid to ask God to help you, whether it's big or small. Talk to Him often. He likes that and wants to help you. You see, I prayed for Bully to come home, and God said, "Okay, Bully, go home." Thanks be to God.

DOING THE RIGHT THING

I met with her before she went in for a heart surgery. We drank some coffee, and she then opened up and shared with me her fear. "I'm not going to make it throught this," she told me. She then said that she had to do it because her children wanted her to. I told her that some fear is always there facing heart surgery. She informed me that she had a dream that was so real, and in it she died.

I had prayer with her, and I felt bad, for I couldn't be there. I had to go to another hospital the next day two hours away for another heart surgery. As I left next morning, I called her and had prayer. After the surgery, I planned to go by to see her on the way home. I found out that her surgery was cancelled because she had a reaction to the anthesisa. "They are doing it in the morning," she said. "You better get ready," she told me. I tried to tell her that she needed to talk to her kids, but she refused. "They want me to have it," she said.

The surgery went well, but that night in the ICU, something went wrong. The nurse called me around 1:00 a.m., and my wife and I went to the hospital. We arrived at the hospital, and she had just died. I wanted to do the right thing, so I trusted her.

Alyssa, when you are faced with doing the right thing, it's not always so easy. As a minister, I knew so many secrets of my members. There was the known but also the unknown. And what was right for me may not be right for them. I always asked God to help me, and He did. What I wanted may not be the right thing. You can be sincere and yet wrong.

People say, "Do the right thing," as if it is some easy task. It's not. I could have told the kids, and many would agree that would have been the right thing. You see, I trusted her; and with God's help, I did the right thing.

GROOM GOES DOWN

The wedding was set for 5:00 p.m. at the church I served. The rehearsal went good the night before, and everybody was ready. We gathered waiting for the bridal march at 5:00 p.m., and the organist started playing it. Everybody came out and took their spot. I came in with the groom and best man.

Everything went normal until the father gave the bride away. I saw the groom begin to sway, and finally he sat down. We had two paramedics, and they came forward to assist the groom. He tried to stand but couldn't. I asked the bride if she wanted to continue, and she said, "Yes." The service continued with the bride standing and the groom sitting.

I pronounced them man and wife, and the best man helped the groom up, and off they went down the aisle.

Alyssa, crazy things can happen at any time in life. This could have been a disaster, but they had the right attitude. Having the right attitude can make or break you. A wrong or bad attitude can destroy you.

When the groom went down, it could have been a disaster, but they kept it together. They were just as married with only one standing instead of two. Make the most of any situation life throws at you, even if it knocks you down.

WILL THE REAL MRS. ELMA STAND UP

I got a call from the funeral home that Mrs. Elma had died. The family wanted me to have the service at the funeral home with visitation before the service. They wanted me to handle it, for I knew what she wanted. They said they would see me at the visitation.

My wife and I showed up early for the visitation and talked with the funeral director, Tom. My wife said she wanted to go see Mrs. Elma. She walked away from us, and after a short time, I heard her say, "This is not Mrs. Elma." We walked around by the casket, and Tom said, "It is Mrs. Elma, I embalmed her." Looking in the casket, I realized it wasn't the Mrs. Elma I knew. I questioned Tom about the family and found out I didn't know these people. Now I had a funeral eulogy all lined up, but one problem—wrong Mrs. Elma. "What are you going to do?" Tom asked. "I'll get to know her when the family gets here," I replied.

So I mingled in the crowd asking bits of information from each of them and put together the eulogy in my head. After the funeral, so many of the family thanked me, even to go so far as saying, "You really knew her."

Alyssa, get to know people. Now you can't get to know them by phone or text or Facebook, you get to know people by talking with them face-to-face. The electronic devices kill communication. You need to watch the person. Are they listening? Can they just sit and talk, or do they have to keep playing with their crutch, the phone? When you take time to listen to someone, you learn a lot. Even though the first time I met her was in the casket. I got to know Mrs. Elma through conversation.

SING ME HOME

etty was one of those outgoing friendly ladies in the church I served. She had served on various state committies, and the plaques were on the wall. Life had been good for Betty.

One day after a doctor's visit, she called me to her home. The news wasn't good, for Betty had cancer, and little could be done. I watched her move from walking to a wheelchair as the cancer sapped the life out of her.

I had many visits with her preparing her for death. She would talk of her faith, and then we would pray together. I remember the first time of praying, I got surprised. She had a wired-up terrier named Pal. While I started praying, he took a flying leap up into Betty's lap while I held her hand. He was close enough to lick me across the nose while I was praying. Betty and I had a good laugh about that, and I learned to keep one eye opened as I prayed for Betty.

Betty had to be moved to a convalescence home. I went to see her, and on one occasion, she told me that she wanted me to sing her home as she died. I had sung a song in church entitled "Beulah Land," and she wanted me to sing it as she died. She also told me that she would let me know when it was time.

It was a Sunday around 5:00 a.m. when she called. My wife answered the phone, and Betty said, "Tell Matt it's time." I got ready and went to the convalescence home to be with Betty. She was conscious for a while, and her kids and husband got to tell her goodbye. She began to drift in and out of consciousness, and she whispered, "It's time." The song that she requested was the song by Squire Parson. I started singing "Beulah Land" as I held her hand. The words are as follows:

> I'm kind of homesick for a country,
> To which I've never been before.
> No sad goodbyes will there be spoken,
> For time won't matter anymore.

> *Second Verse*
> I'm looking now just across the river,
> To where my faith shall end in sight.
> Now just a few more days to labor,
> Then I will take my heavenly flight.

> *Chorus*
> Beulah Land, I'm longing for you,
> And one day on thee I'll stand.
> There my home shall be eternal,
> Beulah Land, sweet Beulah Land.

And as I sang the chorus, I felt her grip release, and the nurse came in and said, "She's gone." God's spirit was so alive as I sang her home.

Alyssa, I have helped countless people go home. Death is like an old friend to me always around. But God's spirit is always there, and when a person dies, that's a holy moment. You see, God comes back to take us home. And with family gathered around Betty, I kept my promise and sang her home.

NOTES FROM MARY

ary was a patient on the cancer floor, and her condition was getting worse. As a chaplain, I was beeped to come to her room around 1:00 a.m. I went to the room and greeted her because I had visited her before. She asked me to please sit down. I pulled up a chair by her bed.

We talked some small talk about her condition, and she said the time for her to die was at hand. In fact, she said she would be leaving in the morning, and that's why she called me. "I have some things I need you to tell my three daughters," she said. I took out my little notebook and wrote down what I needed to say.

For each daughter, she had certain things she wanted them to know. Each message was extremely private and not for each other's ears. I assured her that only each daughter would hear her word. She labeled what was wrong in their lives and what she was proud of. To each she gave her love.

After she finished, she told me she needed to rest for the trip. "I'll be leaving in the morning," she reminded me. I left her room, and at 5:30 a.m., I was beeped to the cancer floor to find that Mary had died.

I was there when the family came in, and after a time of tears, I met with each daughter. I sat down with each of them and told them what their mom had wanted them to know. I gave each the notes I took down.

Alyssa, let me tell you what I want you to know:

1. Always tell the truth
2. Always do what's right
3. Look for the good in everyone
4. Help those in need
5. Laugh often, don't make life so serious
6. Know that I love you
7. Know I'm proud of you
8. Finally, talk to God often

And this is my Mary note to you!

Matthew Rucker

ROLL HER OVER

I did a year as a hospital chaplain at a large Level Four Trauma Center in the upstate of South Carolina.

My job was to visit hospital patients, help the family in the death of a loved one, and be part of the trauma team for the emergency room. I loved this job and got to know a lot of the staff and on occasion helped them with personal problems.

It was about 3:00 a.m., and I got a call for a death. Going to the room I met the daughter and son-in-law. Now my responsibility was to get information on a contact person and funeral home to be used. When I asked the questions, the daughter said I would have to wait for her sister because she was the strong one in the family. She said she would be coming in the morning. I told her to come to the emergency room and ask them to beep Matt (the chaplain).

Around 9:00 a.m., I got a call that she had arrived at the hospital. I met her in the ER and got the information about her dad. She then informed me that she wanted to see her dad. I said, "Give me a few minutes to set it up."

Now the setup required going to the morgue, rolling him in front of a viewing glass. The daughter was a large girl, and her husband was like skin and bones. I took them into the viewing room. It is a small room with pull-down chairs on the wall and a large glass window on the facing wall. I stepped up to the window, put my arm around her shoulders, and then I pulled the curtain. She stood there for a moment, and then she threw her arms back, knocking me down, and then fell on top of me.

When she knocked me down, I rolled under those chairs. I couldn't move. I told her husband, "Roll her over, roll her over." He kept patting her hand, and I kept telling him to roll her over. My thoughts were, *What if someone came into the room?* I worked my knees into her back and finally pushed her over. I called for medical assistants and told them she just fainted, not the full story. Later on I did mention about the safety factor of those chairs to the head nurse. She agreed and had them removed.

It wasn't until years after the ER head nurse retired that I shared my story with her. I thought she would die laughing. She also told me she was wondering how I had come up with the recommendation to have the chairs removed as a safety hazard.

Alyssa, never assume what people may do in a crisis situation. I have had gentle people when an accident occurs and death is a result—put their fist through the wall in the family waiting room. Be careful thinking you fully know a person, you never do.

ZACK LETS ME UP

Zack was our first bull born on the home place. His mom couldn't have him, so my wife and I had to pull him. She finally delivered, and my wife blew in his nose and cleaned out his mouth. She continued to blow in his nose and beat his side, and he finally breathed. Welcome to our world, Zack.

Zack grew up fast and became the herd bull for ten years. He now had grown from sixty pounds at birth to two thousand pounds now. He was a good bull.

After the years, his hooves started braking down, and we had to sell him. That was a hard decision to make.

I put him in the corral. It was hard for him to walk. The day for him to go to the market came, and I told the truck driver I would load him. I had taken care of him all these years making sure he had food and water. He knew me, and that would make loading easier.

I got in the pen and headed him to the chute to load. I have a series of gates that close behind the closer you get to the loading chute. I closed the last gate, and Zack stopped. He wasn't going on the trailer. His weight now was twenty-four hundred pounds, and that's a lot of power. He slammed into the gate, which I was standing behind, and knocked it off the pins and slammed me on the ground. Zack was over me, his head just inches from my chest as I lay on my back. I was looking right into his eyes thinking he's going to mash me into the ground. The driver and my wife were screaming, and I couldn't move. His nose touched me, and he backed up. I slowly got up, and Zack loaded on the trailer.

Alyssa, this was a close call. He could have easily ended my life, but he didn't, for I believe God was involved. But I also believe animals remember, and because we gave him life and I took care of him, he gave me life. There is no reason he should have stopped from pushing me in the ground.

Be good to your animals and take care of them. Let them feel and see your love for them. Who knows, one day they may return the favor, just as the day Zack let me up. Thank You, Jesus.

Matthew Rucker

SOMEONE SAVED MY LIFE

It was a regular school day, and I would drop my son off at school. Today I had to go to Columbia to take my mom to the doctor. We arrived at school, and before Brandon got out, he looked at me and said, "Dad, I love you." I responded, "I love you too!" He said, "No matter what happens, I love you!" I responded, "I love you more, always remember that." Brandon added, "Dad, you are a cool dad." With that he got out of the truck. I left for Columbia.

It was getting dark as I approached home. I tried to call him, but no answer. I figured he was next door playing with the boy next door. Arriving at the house, it was dark. I went in cutting on the lights. I noticed the light was on in the computer room, so I headed back down the hall. When I came to the door, I saw him on the floor. I screamed and fell on my knees by him. I tried to pick him up, but he was so stiff. I tried to blow into his mouth, but he was hard to hold. I kept thinking, *This can't be happening.*

All I could think about was him being by himself. I had to go with him. I started saying, "Hang on, Brandon, I'm coming." Going to the closet, I got my gun and loaded it as I kept saying,

"I'm coming." I placed the gun in my mouth, and there was no fear. I knew what I had to do. I was going to be with my son.

Just as I was about to pull the trigger (and I would have), the phone rang. Out of response, I answered it. It was my wife, and she had called in the nick of time. I wouldn't be here if the phone had not rung.

Alyssa, I believe that God, in the nick of time, pushed Angela to call me. God's perfect timing—I've seen it so many times. In the Bible, we read about Abraham about to sacrifice his son. As the knife is raised, he hears a noise. There in the thicket is a ram. God's timing is so awesome. Alyssa, your granddad wouldn't be here if your grandma Angela hadn't called. You see, someone saved my life that night, and I love her dearly because of it. She is my life, and I thank God for using her to save my life.

MORNING VISITORS

It was a Friday morning, one week after Brandon's death at thirteen. Angela was getting ready for work, and I was still in bed. It was around 6:00 a.m. I was drifting in and out of sleep, and all of a sudden, I was aware Brandon and Dad were standing at the foot of the bed. Brandon spoke and said, "Dad, you were a cool dad, and I love you." Dad spoke and said, "Buckshot (his name for me), take care of Chubby (his name for Mom)"; then they were gone, and I told Angela about it, and she went to work. I thought, *It was just a dream.*

After Angela got home from work, she and I were going to Columbia to spend the weekend with Mother. It was dark when we got there, and we had coffee at the dining room table, then Mom said she needed to tell us something. She said, "I had visitors this morning." I asked, "Who?" And she said, "Your dad and Brandon." Now Mom was blind, and she couldn't see our faces as we sat there. She said, "Your dad said you would take care of me." Then continued that Brandon said, "Don't worry, Nanny, I'm fine."

Both of these visits occurred around 6:00 a.m., one hundred miles apart. No way could we have set this up. Mom and I had morning visitors: my dad and Brandon.

I kept my promise and was right there when Mom went to be with our visitors. I can't help but think that when my time comes, the three of them will show up—Dad, Brandon, and Mother.

MY BROKEN WALKING STICK

It was Saturday morning, and my wife and I headed to the flea market. We had been informed that there was a man there who fixed walking sticks. I had broken mine and getting it fixed was the big agenda for the day.

Arriving at the flea market, we asked around a while, but no one knew of a walking stick man. Disappointed, we left the market, thinking it was a dead-end trip.

We headed home, and my wife goes out to my sister-in-law's shop to do bookwork. While she was there, a friend of ours, Greg, comes in for lunch. She mentions the walking stick, and he says, "Let me have it." He leaves with the stick and later comes back with it fixed. She asks how much she owed him, and he said, "Nothing, glad to do it."

You see, my plan for the day got nixed that morning, but God—in His desire to answer a prayer—gets it done. My walking stick was fixed.

Alyssa, this story reminds me of something my grandmother told me. She said she prayed to God that I would accept Jesus Christ as my Savior before I entered the Air Force. She felt that if I didn't, then I sure wouldn't after I got in. But it was while in the Air Force that I accepted Jesus as my Savior. You see, God didn't answer Granny's prayer but answered the desire of her heart.

I prayed that the man would be at the flea market, but he wasn't, yet God answered the desire of my heart to get my stick fixed.

Remember, when you pray, it may not happen as you think. Give it to God, and trust He will work it out—no matter how small the request, such as fixing a walking stick.

MY BEER BUDDY

He was a big man who would not allow anyone to get too close. As a church member, he was friendly but never close. We were casual to each other as minister and parishioner.

One day I had to go to Sam's Club to get some supplies. When I parked my truck to go in, I noticed a shopping cart with a case of Corona beer left in it. I walked past it and went in to get my supplies. When I came out, the beer was still there by my truck. It was getting hot outside, so I put it in my truck not knowing what I would do with it. I headed home. Arriving back in our little town, I stopped by the cafeteria for lunch. I sat down with Neal. We talked, and I thought I would give the beer to him. "Neal, I have something for you, but I need to go to your shop to give it to you." He said he would follow me there. When we got to the shop, I got out and asked him, "Do you like foreign beer?" He answered, "Some." So I gave him the case of Corona beer. He was shocked and finally said, "I never had a preacher give me a case of beer." I told him to enjoy it and left.

After that instance, he and I became close. He would see me at the cafeteria and ask if I could come by the shop to talk. He shared personal problems and theological ones. We always had good talks, and his faith grew. He began to hug me and kiss me on the cheek. He became one of my best friends.

We were both kind of crazy, and one incident, the church remembered, was at his son's wedding, which I officiated. He and I danced together, laying my head on his chest. We had become best friends.

I was called to let me know my friend had died. They wanted me to do his funeral. This was the last gift I could give my friend. At the funeral, I shared this story with the people, which was a large crowd. No one knew the story except Neal and I.

Alyssa, I never had a beer buddy except here. Neal knew I didn't judge him, but just wanted to be friends. You never know how giving a gift to someone can affect your life or theirs. Never in my wildest dreams did I know how a case of beer could affect my life in gaining a true friend. Now, don't go out and buy the beer, but if it is presented to you, use it in the right way. Who knows, you may gain a beer buddy.

KICKING A DEAD DOG

Mr. and Mrs. Smith lived alone with no children. They were up in years now, and Mr. Smith wasn't doing good healthwise, and I went to see them. Now, Mrs. Smith was always so negative about things. She was sitting on the porch when I arrived, and I sat with her and listened to her talk about Mr. Smith. Everything was just so bad, she kept saying.

As I listened, Matt came up with the idea to try and cheer her up. Sitting on her porch on that beautiful spring day, I began my plan. "Isn't it a beautiful sunny day?" I said. She answered, "Yes, but you can get cancer from the sun." Pausing a moment, I tried again, "Your lawn is so green and beautiful," trying to cheer her again. "Yes, but you have to hire someone to cut it," she responded. Not giving up, I saw a robin in the yard, and I added, "Well, isn't that one of the prettiest robins you have ever seen?" She looked at me and said, "Yes, but he craps all over my clothes on the clothesline." That ended my cheer-up plan.

Alyssa, you can't cheer some people up. In trying, they will bring you down. I always tried to visit a positive person after a negative one. It seemed to balance it out.

Remember, you can't make a person happy. They have to find it within themselves. If you try, they will pull you down, and life will become miserable. When you try many times, as we say on the farm, "You're kicking a dead dog."

GROWING OLD IS HELL

I visited a ninety-four-year-old church member. She was sitting in her favorite chair, and I sat down on the couch next to her. We talked about her family and her health. Using the button to raise the chair, she came up and said, "You know something, preacher?" I leaned forward and said, "What's that, Mrs. D?" She responded, "You got to be tough as hell to grow old." I never forgot that because it is true.

Alyssa, growing old is tough. I live with pain every day. I have a bad shoulder and two bad legs. They have become as old friends. The pain never leaves. What I have done to help is learn to adjust. I adjust my life in what I can do. I can't climb ladders, or stairs, or take long walks.

It is very frustrating when I can't do what I used to do. But I have to adjust and allow others to help me. Thank God for my friends. Friends become so important as we grow old. Also, thank God for my faith that gets me through every new day. Yes, growing old is hell, but knowing that there is nothing I and God can't handle is helpful.

So, Alyssa, enjoy doing things while you can, for one day, you will realize that it is hell growing old. Work on your faith and develop new friends for that time.

AN OLD FRIEND

Alyssa, I have been asked numerous times if I were afraid of death. Let me share what I tell people.

Death has always been a part of my life in the ministry. I have dealt with it hundreds of times. From the very young to the very old, the healthy to the unhealthy, it has come. It keeps showing up like an old friend.

Death comes to us all. To some it comes quietly in the middle of the night. To some it comes quickly and unexpected. To others it comes through much pain and suffering. However it comes, it comes to us all. At the present it is running at 100 percent per person. Now death can be seen as the enemy, but it's really our friend. I think of death as the anesthesia that God gives us when we change bodies. It becomes a doorway to an eternal land called heaven.

When I talk with my science friends, I share a story. My background is science, and logic and probability is a part of that. So I tell them, "If both of us die right now and there is no life after death, who loses?" They reply, "No one." I then say, "But what if there is life after death, who loses?" They usually remain silent, and I respond, "You do." I encourage them to "play the odds, don't take a chance."

Alyssa, I said death has always been a part of my life, it always comes around. So when my time comes and death shows up, I will smile and say, "Welcome, old friend."

THE CROSS IN ME

Alyssa, most of my life was and is dedicated to serving God, helping people, and to be the best person that I can be. The Cross is a symbol of my faith, love, and devotion to Jesus Christ.

The Cross has been there for me when the hard times of life came, such as my divorce, the death of Brandon, and now my health. What keeps me going is the assurance that God is with me and that He loves me.

I have tried to instill this in countless numbers of people that I have served as their minister, helping them through their own hard times. It amazes me how God works in situations, and I thank Him each day for His presence in my life.

Your faith is the most important thing in your life. Yes, even more so than a horse. I wish for you a strong faith as you mature, and remember, your reputation will make or break you in this life, so become somebody.

You will find that life takes no prisoners, and hard times will come your way, it does to everyone. The most important thing when hard times come will be your attitude. You can fall on the floor and cry, "Poor pitiful me," get mad at the whole world, or square your shoulders and face it—whatever it is.

Always remember, you never solve anything by running away, you have to face it no matter how painful.

My prayer is that you will find that faith and lean on God. There is nothing you and God can't handle, for that has always been true in my life.

My faith has carried me from Sandy Run to all over the United States and the jungles of South America. And with this I have friends all over the world, for people see my faith and know that I am real. I am who I am because God has had His hand on my life.

So know that God will always be there and I am always close by. I am proud of you, and I pray for you each night, and so hold on to the truth that God is always close by.

EPILOGUE

Alyssa and dear friends, I hope with these short stories that you know more about me as a person. That I remained true to my faith, tried to help people along the way and I was a bit of a rascal. I have enjoyed every minute of life.

My aim was to also give you tidbits of wisdom that I learned going through each situation. Hopefully it will be helpful in your life if you face similar situations. Each story was intended not only to make you laugh or cry, but help you think.

My prayer is that your wisdom level moved up some. May God continue to bless you and remember to learn to laugh. There is not one shred of evidence to prove that life is serious, we make it serious. So share your story. Everybody has a story. Share your story and God will bless you and others.

Matthew D. Rucker

CPSIA information can be obtained
at www.ICGtesting.com
Printed in the USA
JSHW020229220720
6794JS00002B/51